Thrive or Survive

Tips on Choosing the Life <u>You</u> LOVE to Live

NICOLE MCLAREN CAMPBELL

DEDICATION

To my instafriends who share their triumphs and struggles and inspire me to share what I have learned
To all who have enriched my journey by helping me to choose - Nicola my most unreasonable friend, Jeffrey my
best friend, my sisters and sister friends,
My parents,
My team at work and home
My children - I THRIVE for you!

CONTENTS

WHY CHOOSE

We were not placed on this earth to eat, work, sleep, repeat. That is mere survival. We were placed on this earth to THRIVE and it is ALL a choice. Thank you to my most unreasonable friend Nicola for reinforcing this so many times that I CANNOT forget it. The moment we view our lives as a choice - the good, the bad, the ugly - we take control of it. "If you don't like where you are, move, you are not a tree" - one of my favorite quotes and so incredibly apt. Now, warning, you might resist this - it's our brains natural reaction to an idea that goes against what we've always thought or held onto, an idea that threatens our safety or identity. But, try it on, please.

To warm you up and get you ready for what is to come, here is a choosing exercise I first did at the Landmark Forum - speak these words out loud (force yourself to if you must, but do it!):

I choose my bank account balance.
I choose my credit card debt.
I choose my weight.
I choose my husband and children.
I choose his children.
I choose the mother of his children.
I choose my family.
I choose my home.
I choose my car.
I choose my friends.
I choose my job.
I choose my boss.
I choose my clients.
I choose my salary.
I choose, I choose, I choose.

Repeat.

The exercise above transformed my life after I had my first child, my baby LC. I was overwhelmed and although undiagnosed I am convinced that I was suffering from post-partum something. The anxiety was unbearable. I felt such pressure to build a business that hadn't near gotten off the ground and I had no team. My marriage was also brand new. I felt like I had to be the best mom and I felt I always got it wrong. Not having enough breast milk seemed like the evidence of my insufficiency. It was ROUGH. I cried so much. And then I did the choosing exercise at the Landmark Forum. I revisited the exercise today as I was heading to the airport, feeling overwhelmed and scattered and anxious, a bit resentful of someone on my team that I thought I was helping so much, who wasn't trying to help me. Then, I chose it all. I chose all the circumstances that brought about those feelings. I recognized my own choices and reactions and I said "I am responsible" and no one owes me anything. Whatever I do, I choose.

Such a feeling of power and energy and peace came over me all at the same time!

So, I urge you to choose. Breakdown, build up, laugh, cry, get angry or frustrated or resentful or bitter, feel sorry for yourself - then choose. Whatever you aren't happy with you choose to leave or choose to change your view of it and reaction to it. It sounds so simple, right? I've found that life is pretty simple. We overcomplicate it and confusion, fear or fear masked as confusion become our greatest reason or excuse. The hard truth is that, most of the time, we know what we need to do. It's the action we need to take. It's the courage we have to build.

This book is about helping you to work out how to choose more, choose to build the courage and choose to take action. I want you to think deeply, and treat this like a workbook - mark it up, highlight and scribble - if you have really done the work this book calls you to do, the book should NOT remain pristine.

Your life is your greatest masterpiece, choose now to do the work on it!

1
CHOOSING YOU.

Choosing YOU is the first chapter and it is the first chapter on purpose. I believe that we find ultimate meaning and fulfillment when we dedicate ourselves to something outside of ourselves, a higher cause, in service to the world. However, it is simply not possible to serve at 100% unless we are at 100%. For that reason I believe that self-care is not the selfish way, it is the ONLY way. You at 100% serves your family, you at your best self serves the world. Be aggressive about choosing yourself, because you are WORTH it and your goals depend on it.

In my visionboard exercise I invite participants to visualize the person they love the most in this world. To further imagine ALL they want for this person. Then, I ask them to want the same for themselves. We must want the same joy and fulfillment for ourselves that we would want for the person we love most in the world. We must choose that for ourselves. Ultimately, we must learn to treat ourselves as we would our most beloved.

So many, women in particular, feel guilty for saying "no" or putting themselves first, time spent on self-care could be spent getting more work done, with children or husband they say, and to that I say that I've learned that my household vibrates off my frequency and energy, to have my best energy I have to take very good care of myself FIRST. My bad mood or great energy will affect my children, my husband, and everything else! When we don't put ourselves first we run the risk of becoming resentful of others who don't put us first. I've learned it's not their job. If I don't put me first who is going to do it for me? No one. It is my responsibility to put me first. It is not my husband, my boss, my kids or my friends job, it is MY job.

So how do you choose you? Where do you start? Start by considering when you feel your best.

What are your YOU-enhancers – the things, people, actions and / or situations that make you feel 'winning' and high energy?

_____

_____

_____

_____

_____

Self-love will push you to surround yourself with people who also love you, and distance yourself from behaviors, people and situations that do not serve you or build you up. Choosing YOU and your best energy means considering when you feel your worst. So, it may be the right time for a life-audit!

What are your YOU-detractors – the things, people, actions and / or situations that make you feel 'losing' and low energy?

_____

_____

_____

_____

_____

_____

Some of the ways I feel my best are: when I am rested, organized, look my best and have my mind on positive. I feel best when I have exercised, am eating well and have a plan. I feel like a winner when I am crushing my goals and making progress in the direction of my vision. I feel my best when I am spending quality time with my children and husband. So, I choose me by building in more of the above into my schedule, making them as much of a lifestyle as possible. When I say building them into my schedule, I mean entering appointments for self into my calendar. Yes, it's that serious. If it doesn't get calendared it doesn't get done (for me anyway!). Routine is my best friend when it comes to choosing me. I have routines with my kids to ensure we get quality time, and I hit repeat on those daily or weekly e.g. bedtime stories, Sunday dinners etc. If I don't do these as a part of our lifestyle and routine I will look up and my children will be grown!

I wasn't always this way about building my bests into my routine – and my good friend Yolande, or YoliCess as I call her, put me in check one day when she saw me looking harassed and harried at my manicure appointment – I was running late because I had tried to "fit it in" between two meetings. YoliCess told me, yes told not advised, to set standing appointments, pointing out that I was always running around stressing myself out unnecessarily. I thought about it and realized she was completely right, I love having my nails and toes done, it helps me to feel put together, and when I feel put together I function better. Thus, Fix Up Friday was born. Choosing YOU is about self-care, and self-care is about self-love. As Cleo Wade puts it, "if self-love says 'I love you.' Self-care say, 'Prove It'". Still, I felt incredibly guilty – was I being shallow? What if I really didn't have the time and was compromising my work? I felt so bad! But you know what was worse, looking down at my hands and toes and feeling like a hot mess. It put me in a bad mood. My bad mood affects my husband, children, staff, clients, and of course, myself. Plus, as a public speaker and consultant me not looking put together does affect my business! Who wants to take advice from someone who looks like they don't have it together? Boom! My justification was complete – my Fix Up Friday standing appointment became pro-productivity! If you need to, find the justification for yourself. What matters is that you take an action, do it, try it on, and when you get used to it you will see the benefits and you won't be able to stop! You will do it, just for you, and be perfectly ok with that, I promise. When you choose you, everything around you will flourish - your relationships, your business, your finances - everything!

Some of the other ways I practice self-care as a lifestyle is by exercising at a specific time, daily, when I KNOW that no husband (ok not always LOL), no kids, no AIM parent, no client will need to reach me for any purpose. I eat energy inducing food which I plan 1 week in advance for the week to come. I give myself a break by delegating things that don't bring me joy, or that I don't HAVE to do. I choose ME by using my lunch times to decompress, whenever possible. I do admit, most of my lunches are working lunches, but more and more I am learning to choose me by going for a walk, alone, during lunch. Claim that time – if you make sure that your working time is super focused and productive, you can take that one hour for you and treat it as sacred.

Consider your You-Enhancers, how can you make them a part of your lifestyle? I described my standing appointments and calendaring above, my sister Rachel keeps a self-care jar -for birthdays and Christmas gifts she asks for spa treatments, then she saves them up and uses them throughout the year. I love that strategy! time.

What's your WHY for making your YOU-enhancers part of your lifestyle?

_____

_____

_____

_____

_____

_____

List some ways you can make self-care, practicing your YOU-enhancers an integrated part of

your lifestyle.

_____

_____

_____

_____

_____

_____

On what days / times will you practice or integrate these YOU-enhancers?

_____

_____

_____

_____

_____

Now, let's talk about your YOU-detractors. The habits, people, actions, situations that make you feel 'pop-down', drained or low-energy. Say "I am responsible". Now that we have taken responsibility, let's shift.

Of the YOU-detractors you listed above, write the ones that are in your control below and note how you can stop / reduce them. What YOU-enhancers can you replace the YOU-detractors with? *Hint – change especially when it comes to habit is easier when you start small and replace worsts with bests as opposed to focusing on eliminating the bads!*

Can't control it? Well, you are 100% responsible for how you react. Don't choose frustration and anger. Change your mindset by seeing it from another perspective – easier said than done right? Do the exercise below, dig deep, to see how you can shift your perspective.

For each of your YOU-detractors, list what the person / situation could be here to teach you? Can you be grateful for the lesson?

_____

_____

_____

_____

_____

When it comes to frustration, when the lesson isn't enough to shift my mood I turn on some winning music and sing OUT LOUD (I have an entire playlist of boosters – see thriveorsurvivethebook.com for the deets!).

Self-care, I'm learning (slowly), is also about knowing when to pull back and choose rest. I learned to drop the guilt and take care of myself, in terms of my exercise, hair, nails, spa dates but I am still learning when it comes to slowing down and actually RESTING. I think this is where the "know thyself" rule comes in. I am very driven by practicality and usage of time that produces results. How I spend my time and what I do has to make sense to me in a way that is tied to my overall vision and goals, and this is the way I will stick to decisions or new habits. With rest, I tell myself that it is an investment in my productivity and the results I produce. Rest is an investment in my energy level, which is also tied to my results AND the quality of my relationships. If I am in a good mood, or have winning energy I get more done, build better relationships in business, and I am a nicer person to my kids, husband, employees and anyone I interact with. I have learned to apply that results-based mindset to rest, to prayer, to reading my Bible, to these things that don't show on the outside but give me such peace and winning on the inside.

Sometimes though, I try to rest and my mind races with all the things I need to do and I feel as though I am wasting time when I could be smashing goals. Now, I am learning to listen to my inner voice, and the more I pray the louder my inner voice gets. It tells me when I shouldn't go to the gym, it tells me when I need to take a day. It tells me when I need to write down a list and a plan and take immediate action on ONE of the million things I have to do, or when I need to write the list, plan and then sleep. Or, when I just need to sleep! I now observe myself and my energy levels and mood very carefully. I know that if I work 7 days a week I will NOT be able to work even a 5 day week the following week. When I get miserable, short tempered, pessimistic or sad … I know it's time to rest! I know what is going to happen if I don't take a complete break.

When do you KNOW it is time to rest? Write 3 indicators below.

_____

_____

_____

I know that if I don't rest, I will have a meltdown, there will be many tears, a headache and I won't be able to do anything creative or productive for at least 2 days. "It will be traumatic Nicole", is what I tell myself!

Describe what happens when you do not rest.

_____

_____

I am at my BEST Mon-Fri when I get 7-8 hours of sleep. It means I have to TURN OFF the Instagram after the kids have gone to bed. I talk to people with all kinds of different schedules and responsibilities - the truth is that we need a certain amount of sleep to function best - we all do. I suggest starting with trying to get 10 minutes more sleep, and build slowly. More sleep means more focus during my work hours, but it means I have to really be focused and maximize the time. I have to go HARD! I am at my best when my Saturday's belong to me, there is no plan or schedule or 'Must Do' - I might go for a drive with Jeffrey, we might go to visit friends or I might hang out with my girlfriends, supervise my kids' sleepovers or just hang out with them. When my entire Sunday is devoted to laying in bed, binge watching Power or Homeland, reading a lovely frivolous romance novel, chatting with friends, playing board games with my kids, watching movies and not leaving home, I feel ready for the week ahead, then I will plan my week ahead on Sunday evenings.

The real world of my businesses and life means that this does not always happen (especially on a Saturday), but I know that being off, to reset my brain is how I will work best Mon-Fri so I do my very best to have my weekends. I don't like going to get my hair done on a Saturday, or running errands – so I automate as much as possible between Fontana, Supermarket, Amazon – I set up systems to make these as pain free, easy and quick as possible (more on this in the chapter on Choosing Support) so I can truly have my weekends. Sundays however are sacred and I can probably count on one hand (ok 2!) how many times in a given year I work on a Sunday. And if I do, I need Monday or Wednesday off. I learn to pull back from experience - the painful consequence of not listening to my inner voice. I know how I feel when a total meltdown is coming, and I know what the meltdown will mean – I will cry, feel sad, hopeless and be unable to do anything. I will be terribly anxious. I know how much time it will take for me to get back to the real me. Because I have experienced the painful consequences of not pulling back, I am better about listening to my inner voice and resting when I need to.

When I pull back during the week I feel anxious about what I'm not getting done, so my pull back needs to happen on the weekends and that is why I protect them so fiercely. On Monday I am refreshed and ready to win! But let me tell you, on the days I work is not a kinda sorta work it's a go HARD kinda work. Choosing rest means you choose productivity. I am motivated to maintain complete focus during the day, because getting more work done in work time gives me back more time for rest and family and simple me time.

By doing that, I am pacing myself and I am choosing ME.

How can you design your schedule so that you get enough sleep and rest?

_____

_____

_____

_____

_____

_____

Self-care is also about practicing self-compassion. I must admit that self-compassion doesn't come readily to me, I am often the hardest person on myself. At the start of 2018 I decided that I would focus on being kinder to myself, to reduce my stress levels and because I love myself! You see, I drive myself SO HARD and had this perverse guilt when I wasn't, that it started to produce counterproductive results and epic meltdowns which interfere with my happiness. I really believe that we are meant to be happy in this life, and that life is a journey and we have to practice self-compassion to truly enjoy the journey - the ups and downs, the wins and losses, the bumpy bits and the smooth parts - they are all a part of it, and without self-compassion the downs, losses and bumps are too debilitating. So, now, I forgive myself more easily. I don't shy away from the lesson (we NEED to learn the lesson to do better, so this is not about letting ourselves off the hook), but I literally speak to myself, saying things like "it's OK Nicole, next time you will know better and do better", "you've still come a far way, it's a process", "don't worry everyone makes mistakes", "even the most epic people have failed, you're not immune", "rest a bit" etc.

Do you practice self-compassion?
How do you speak to yourself when you make a mistake or when something goes wrong?
Would you speak to someone you loved in that way if the same thing happened to them?

The next time you make a mistake, instead of beating yourself up, what will you say to yourself instead?

_____

_____

Choosing ME is about feeding my spirit and investing in myself. It's about really loving me. Choosing YOU is not static, it's a continuous process of up-leveling. It's about thinking of prospective YOU-enhancers – they might not be a part of your life right now but could help you to level UP!

I am working on more regularly investing in myself in terms of self-development / skills building, spending more time with people I can learn from, reading more etc. I'm working on cutting procrastination, emotional eating, over working myself, lack of self-compassion, not spending enough time with my parents etc. It's a daily process. Decide to do it. You absolutely must spend more time on introducing and building more of the life enhancers and reducing and eliminating the detractors if you hope to build the life you LOVE to live. This is part of what it means to choose YOU.

2
CHOOSING RELATIONSHIPS

I am CHOOSING to talk about relationships now because so many have asked and because, without words of experience and wisdom from others I would be so far behind in so many areas of my life! I can't allow fear or fear of what others might think to hold me back. That would go against the very essence of what I teach and what I believe. Please also know that I am not positioning myself as an expert or authority ... I simply wish to share my experience and what I have learned from older, more seasoned women.

So many men and women (mostly women) have shared their situation-ships seeking guidance. In most cases the mistake happens we don't know ourselves enough to know what kind of person will help us, and who we can help, to grow and maximize potential. Then we choose what does not serve us, emotions get involved and we find ourselves deeply wrapped in situations we really had no business being in in the first place. We knew they weren't right or couldn't work ... but, we chose them anyway. I've been there!

When I met Jeffrey, I was becoming clearer and clearer about who I was, and what I wanted for my life in the long-term and how I wanted to serve the world. I was clear in my mind that I needed someone who could help me to be more of who I was called to be. I wanted to help this person be more of who he was called to be too - I wanted that partnership. During the early stages of our relationship I was introduced to Visionboarding. This is when I really got SUPER clear about what I wanted for my future, in all areas, wrote it down and put the images on the board. This was life-changing for me, because it put me mentally in the driver's seat. Visionboarding made me a chooser. I wanted marriage and children. I wanted my husband to be a strong leader, which would mean he would have to be smart so I could respect his judgement even when it disagreed with my own. I got very clear that I wanted someone who took family seriously. All of those things I put on my Visionboard.

In all decisions, not just with relationships, I find myself constantly going back to my why - and I urge you to consider your why.

What it is that you want to do and who do you want to be in this world?

Write what comes to mind when you think - How will the world be different because I have lived?

_____

_____

_____

_____

These are the questions that I ask myself, that informed the very clear formulation of my mission and vision for my life. I wrote it down: _My mission is to help as many people as possible awaken to their infinite possibilities and maximize their potential._

You should write it down too, right here, right now.

My mission is to _____

_____

Based on my mission I knew I needed someone who believed that the mission was worthy and important, who deeply believed I was capable of accomplishing my mission on a large scale. For me, the values and attitude and mindset were a major key. Initially I chose Jeffrey because our fundamental values aligned so closely. He values family. He is generous. He loves people. He thinks it's important to be a nice person. He loves deeply. He is a protector and a provider. He loves God. He treated his mom really well when she was alive. He's funny, like really funny. We could talk forever. He thinks I can conquer the world and he wants to support me to do just that. He's a big cheerleader for me. When I wanted to start my own business soon after we met, he said "of course you can and you should, now" when I had so much doubt he was 199 percent sure I would make a success of it. He quickly became my best friend. All the serious important stuff of life things I think are important he thinks are important. We are different in so many ways but we see eye to eye on the really key issues we take seriously. In previous relationships I KNEW it wasn't right when the core values were not in alignment. I have such big dreams and such a pull to answer my calling in life, to do so on a large scale, I knew I needed someone who would support that and whose presence in my life would actually fuel me to be one hundred percent who I am called to be. No one is perfect but I needed someone smart and open to change, someone open to new ideas, open to me helping him to grow and able to help me to grow too. I knew that I could not be constantly distracted by drama in my relationship and still be one hundred percent who I am called to be. I deeply wanted to be that person for my partner too.

Relationships are not static, and even the most equally-yoked, uber compatible meant to be together human beings must necessarily experience conflict. The way I see it I experience inner-conflict, conflict with my own self so why wouldn't I experience it with someone else? No relationship is perfect and no human being is - Jeffrey and I do not have a perfect relationship even though he is everything I could have dreamed of and visioned! Marriage is WORK, but we are doing the work and we are both committed to that. Over time you get to know your partner, I try to understand him and his perspective which is so different from mine. People are a function of their culture and background, parents, earliest influences, stuff that has happened in their past, temperaments, belief system etc. I wouldn't want a husband who was just like me that would be a hot mess. So, when those differences cause conflict choosing to communicate honestly, clearly and quickly helps me ALOT. It doesn't matter if he doesn't choose the same, or say sorry as quickly or forgive as easily. I have confidence in who he is as a person. I can only control myself. So, I choose to communicate.

I believe that relationships make our lives. I am very clear that destructive relationships WILL take me off the path of my purpose in life, will prevent me from maximizing my full potential, fulfilling my mission and realizing my vision. That is a price I had to tell myself was just too much to pay. The relentless drama, angst and heartbreak was a NO! When you view the choice of everything, including partner through that lens, it just becomes that serious! Choose wisely.

Given your mission and vision (what you see for yourself), what are some of the most important characteristics of someone who will strengthen you must have?

_____

_____

_____

_____

_____

_____

As you decide on relationships you must think - will this person support, neutralize or detract you from self-actualization? What does self-actualization mean for you? For me it's being happy - healthy and whole relationships with family and friends AND fulfilling my mission 100 percent.
That's my ambition.
I heard once that an ambitious person has two choices - a super supportive partner or no partner at all. I couldn't agree more.

Simply put, you must ask yourself, just what is the life I (would) love to live?

_____

_____

_____

_____

COMMUNICATION

Communication is the MAJOR key choice of a thriving relationship. Choosing superb communication in your relationship means you don't use silence as a weapon. If something Jeffrey says or does affects me in a negative way I tell him, immediately. I try to tell him calmly and clearly … but depending on what it is that doesn't always work LOLLLL but I am working on that too. I could CHOOSE to just get super angry on the inside and ignore him to provoke a reaction but I decided that a harmonious, loving relationship is the outcome I want for myself and my children in the long term. So, things like deliberately extending an argument to punish him, or provoke a reaction or prove how unbothered I am etc., tempting as they are in the moment, I have decided not to do. When he says sorry, I accept it wholly and completely and when I mess up, I just take ownership as quickly as possible. I let go of my need to be right (and ladies you know we are usually right! And being right feels so so so goooood yum yum!). I don't make excuses. I try to understand his feelings. I do it quickly. Because these things pile on top of each other over time and erode relationships. So, I choose to communicate very clearly how something makes me feel and why, and how I would prefer for him to act / be in the future. He doesn't always accept it accept immediately or commit to doing things differently but I know he has heard me. I believe that no matter what there is a love and a respect there so when either of us fall out of line with that, and we are reminded, then we will eventually correct.

Your Partner Cannot Read Your Mind

Ok this may come as a surprise but literally no one can ready your mind! So. I choose to tell Jeffrey what

I want and need because I want and need it and I want to make sure it happens! I am not over here expecting him to read my mind. I don't think it is his job to make me happy. I make myself happy. But if there are things that he can do to bring me joy … I tell him! For example, I love Valentine's Day and dates. Those things are not important to him. When we just started dating Valentine's Day came and left without the slightest acknowledgment - unless it was telling me how ridiculous he found the entire thing. But, since I love it, I make sure he understands they are important to me so … slowly … over time I notice that he asks me out more, and, no matter where he is in the world, I'm getting flowers on Valentine's Day.

I explain to him my ME-enhancers, my non-negotiables like exercise and doing my nails even if when I choose to do those things is not always convenient! Because he understands my why, it no longer provoked resistance when he would rather have me doing something else.

Splitting the Labor

I have some roles and Jeffrey has some - I don't want to deal with house repairs, construction, the yard or the dogs. As my daughter said "Mommy is not THAT kind of mom she doesn't like going outside." He doesn't want to deal with making sure there's food in the house or organizing meals or kids schedules or bedtime routines. Jeffrey just loves to tell me "that's your department"

I no longer resent him not knowing the kids' schedules and events, but when they are happening I tell him and communicate that I expect him to make the effort to be there, whether he feels like it or not. He has his own routines with the kids, like feeding the dogs and doing chores around the house and yard. I respect that. It did take us a while to settle all of that and maybe it's not 50/50 (have you met a Jamaican man?!) but it works for us and when it doesn't work you can be sure I will … You guessed it! I will COMMUNICATE my feelings! The truth is that if you do everything without communicating your partner will assume that you happily have it all under control as your own resentment rises. For me that is a SWERVE!

Each relationship is different, people are different but with open communication and an understanding of your partner it's possible to choose a loving, harmonious supportive relationship most of the time!

One thing Brian Tracy pointed out in terms of communication is asking for feedback. A foreign concept to me in terms of my marriage but having a conversation around - what am I doing that makes you happy, that I could do more of. What am I doing that doesn't make you happy. This single conversation can really change everything!

CHOOSING THE ENTIRE PERSON

Choosing your partner is a daily decision. Choosing your relationship means choosing your person when he or she is WINNING and happy and everything is going great AND when he/she is down and out. Life is peaks and valleys. I depend on Jeffrey so much in my pop down periods. He scraped me up, a crying heap, when I had to face the prospect of giving my first speech to an adult audience. I supported him when he wanted to change direction in his career. I will support him with whatever he feels called to do and I will do so fiercely. Because choosing someone means choosing ALL of them and taking on their growth and development as if your entire life depended on it. You can't make someone happy but once you know what they need you can set about making sure it happens as much as you humanly can.

3
CHOOSING PURPOSE

Please take from my decision to talk relationships that what you have to offer the world is not about you and your fear, it is about how you can serve, how you can use your experiences and insights to light the path for someone else, the way so many peoples' insight and experiences have lit the path for you. I decided I would not allow other people's opinions of who I am, am not, or should be, to interfere with me answering my calling. I would not allow the fear of judgement to cause me to shrink. I learned this in high school, I was titled "nuff" which in Jamaican means "extra" - I asked lots of questions in class because I was so afraid of getting a test and not knowing the answer! It was more important to do well in my exams than to be liked. You must make the decision, right now, that your mission, vision, purpose your BEST life is more important than being liked. Every time I read the quote "You will be too much for some people. Those people are not your people" I think of my high school life, and to be frank, my current life! My high school period in Jamaica was painful yet it made me so strong, because when I hear that I am 'too much' I am unaffected. You know courage is daily action, it is not a thing you learn and that's the end. You have to practice it and keep practicing it until it is a part of you. So, I daily practice the courage to be 100% myself irrespective of how other people feel about it. As long as I am not imposing harm on another, and I feel happy, and I feel purposeful, then I am fine.

At the end of the day we are here to light each others' paths - and use our gifts to do so in which ever ways we can. That's why I've never subscribed to the idea that my life had to be about one thing - that I had to find this one job and do it exclusively until forever. TD Jakes said that if you can't identify your purpose, identify your passions, because passion will lead you to purpose.

So I ask you, if there were no limits and all things were possible, what would you be doing? What are some of the things you just enjoy doing?

_____

_____

_____

_____

_____

_____

Your fears become your limits, and the first step of working through fear is acknowledging that it exists.

So, what are you most afraid of?

_____

_____

_____

_____

I am an eternal optimist but I am not reckless. I am a proponent of choice, but I think carefully, I take risks but they are calculated. So, you might not be doing what you LOVE right now in this moment, but see your current job or source as income as the fund for your dream and put aside as much as you can, deliberately to save toward that dream or invest in that dream. My friend Thione Niang shared with me that when he got very clear about his vision and knew what he needed to do, he had another job offer on the table and he did a calculation of how much it would cost to meet his responsibilities monthly including care of his son, and decided to NOT to follow the passion, but to take the job for the exact number of months he needed to in order to save to ensure that he would still be able to meet his responsibilities for an entire year – when he had that in the bank, he resigned and started to pursue his passion.

Identifying our true passion and walking in purpose involves choice AND planning. It means choosing your NOW and being a boss at that, until you take the bold step in the direction of your dream.

What will you need to do now, in the next 3 months, 6 months, or 1 year in order to prepare yourself to pursue your passion? Beyond saving, what small action(s) can you take daily to build that dream?

_____

_____

_____

_____

_____

I pray daily for the ability to tap into my gifts and strengths to serve - and I don't believe that has to be ONE thing, but at the same time I pray for direction so that I can FOCUS on those things that are of high value. In pursuit of our highest calling, no matter how passionate we are, there will be a cost. It might mean less time, more work, more aggressive investment, it might mean going out less, fewer friends, less free time, feeling uncertain, it might mean exposing yourself to fear, failure and disappointment … what is the price that you will have to pay?

Who do you need to CHOOSE to be?

When I made my first Visionboard I knew I had to CHOOSE to be the exercising type and the salad-eating type because I needed that energy and confidence to fulfill my mission to empower as many people as possible to awaken to their infinite possibilities and fulfill their potential. I had to pay the price - surrendering control (I had to submit to someone else telling me what to do and eat, which I hated!!), I had to pay the price of waking up earlier to exercise, I had to pay the price of experiencing the PAIN of discipline and believe me it was painful. I had to pay the price (literally) of hiring a trainer at the gym to create accountability for myself.

So I ask again, who do you need to CHOOSE to be to fulfill your mission?

_____

_____

_____

_____

What is the price you will have to pay?
Write it down.

_____

_____

_____

_____

Are you willing to pay the price?

Make a pledge to yourself.

On this _____ day of _____ 20__ __, I _____ am willing

to pay the price of

_____

in order to achieve

_____.

When I was tempted to give up I knew that I went back to my why, my mission. I knew deep within that I could not empower others 150% without feeling fully confident myself. I could not meet the calling on my life without my maximum energy. I had to CHOOSE to cut my procrastination and excuses, because my dreams demanded it.

4
CHOOSING YOUR 'ALL' (AND BALANCING IT).

DISCLAIMER: This is a big topic, and this chapter may just turn into it's own book. There are so many facets and aspects of the "can we have it all?" conversation. In this chapter I am skimming the surface, I know (which is why I thought, this may be my next book). But since there can be no conversation on Thriving or Choosing without it, let's talk!

When I just started my business, I worked 7 days a week, from as early as 6:30 am to 11 pm at night. I was the secretary, accountant, tutor, coach and marketer for AIM. Of course, I had no kids and my relationship with my now-husband, then-boyfriend was in its infancy.

Then, I got married and had children.

I made a choice to spend my time differently.

My energy is absorbed and consumed differently now and I simply cannot physically or psychologically work in the same way I did pre-babies and marriage. I am in a season of my life where I have young children. My priority is building a solid, close, loving relationship with them and it requires time. For example, I generally decline invitations, meetings or appointments that take me away from home during the week between 6 and 8 pm, because I want to spend that time with my kids, talking and reading. I actually schedule it – as I type this very sentence it is 5:15 pm and I know I have 45 mins left to work. I have to be strict and aggressive with this rule or else everything else gets in the way and before I know it they are grown and I don't know them. That for me is not an option. I am not willing to pay that price.

Not to mention my relationship with my husband.

Many nights I have work on my mind, and am itching to do it, but Jeffrey wants to hang out and watch a movie - I always choose him. It means the work doesn't get done that night. But, in the end I MUST remember the priority - my family, my relationships. I have to get the work done – and I still do – just not right then and there. This is why I am so passionate about focus and productivity during the times I am working. I do not plan work for home on most nights because I know that it is likely that I will have other family commitments. Small choices add up to big problems (or big wins). I would rather play catch up and figure it out later. Sometimes I think ok in the long-run I accept that I may not (my fingers are itching to type WILL NOT, but I hold on to the hope!) get to the peak or pinnacle of my career, or maximize my career potential in the same time frame that I would have if I had no family, because I just don't put in the same hours that someone else out there does ... and I have come to accept that reality… but I am living my all, my family is my priority. The truth is, I don't want to reach the pinnacle and to be there alone.

Define YOUR 'all'

I am a huge proponent about being DELIBERATE in life - and being unafraid to define your own success, irrespective of what others believe that should look like - in both your personal and professional life. In the previous chapter we talked about Choosing Purpose, now let's consider life in all its glorious possibilities. What is your definition of 'all'? I knew I wanted to get married. I knew I wanted to have children. I think I have always known, at least, I can't remember a time when that was not how I felt. I want to raise confident and happy children and I want to support my husband to be his best self, enjoy his support, and build a legacy together. I want us to all be close, which means spending lots of time together, it means considering what value I can bring to my husband's personal and professional growth and spending the time to do so. I jokingly call myself his assistant sometimes! When his album launch was coming up I worked on it daily, in the evenings on the weekends, in between AIM meetings. I was completely exhausted by the time it was launch time – but it was so worth it because my work made a difference to my husband's success and that is how I have decided to show up as a wife. I make the trade-offs according to my priorities and who I want to be in my priority relationships. My 'all' means fulfilling relationships with my family and friends. I want to live passionately (to do that I need to be happy & healthy!), I want to die with no regrets. That is my all – and I want all of it!

I know many people who do not want to have children. And that is fine too. So how do you define your all? The key is to think deeply about your life and listen to your deep inner knowing. Do not allow your fear to dictate your desire in any respect – career, family, finances, spiritual life etc. Do not decide what you want based on what you think is available to you. The universe is infinite and abundance is YOUR birthright. It's mine too. There is more than enough! I remind myself of this when doubt and fear creep in.

Your 'all', Comparison and Opinions of Others
Comparing myself to others can drain my energy and makes me feel less than, but sometimes it can be a good reality check for me. So when I catch myself doing it I ask myself – "what is your 'all' Nicole?". Sometimes I discover that I am looking unto a situation or person, 'longing' for things that I don't even deeply desire according to my 'all' or my vision / mission. It's that "grass is greener on the other side" trick – so I stop, think about the grass I have and say "Nicole you need to water this grass, that you've chosen, and focus on manifesting the rest of it". This is why I believe it is so important to get to know yourself, your dreams, desires, your 'all', and make your own plan. Otherwise you will blow in whatever direction the wind does, be affected by the opinions and desires of others for your life (close, well-meaning people that love you even), never steering your own ship. Anxiety, confusion and unhappiness will result. I have been there. When I finished college, many thought that I should remain in the United States to work because I could earn more and save. I did not want to do that, at all. I desperately wanted to return to Jamaica, I wanted to work and live in Jamaica, raise my family in Jamaica and make a contribution to Jamaica's development -from Jamaica. I know many other people who do not choose that. Members of a diaspora can contribute immensely to their home country's development and indeed members of the Jamaican diaspora are a significant driver in Jamaica's prosperity - their contribution is huge. But I knew what I wanted for MY life, and it started and ended with living in Jamaica. My father, God bless him, didn't agree and it was hard to not have his complete support in my next move. He was afraid for me – a fear borne out of love. Many others were skeptical – soon after I returned to Jamaica I ran into someone in the bathroom and they excitedly asked "You're back in Jamaica? What are you doing now?", to which I even MORE excitedly replied "I'm helping kids get into college!" Excitement replaced by incredulity, he said "You went to Princeton and THAT is ALL you're doing?" I'm not sure how I responded, something muted as I rushed to get away, hoping he could not see the doubt and sadness in my eyes. Luckily those feelings didn't last because I had already created my Visionboard, put myself in the driver's seat of my life, and I knew that I found helping students' to access college deeply fulfilling! I thought, if he knew what to do with a Princeton degree, he should have just gone to Princeton himself! But, he didn't … I did, and I get to say what I want to do with my life! It is an exciting freedom once you embrace it – but first, you must define your all and put yourself in the

driver's seat of your life!

Your dream is your dream for a reason, your all is your all, and no one should be expected to believe in it, or you, more than you! Even the people who love you most in the world and want the best for you can only operate from their own frames of reference and inner-most beliefs and possibilities. You feel what you feel on your heart, and you are responsible for it. What a BLESSING it is to be in control of our own lives, to be able to design and redesign according to our own definitions and heart's desires.

Write down your personal definition of 'ALL' for your life

_____

_____

_____

_____

_____

_____

Once we define, we must design BOLDLY. Too many of us are half in, half out, we never put our full energy behind our deepest desires, but rather we settle for what someone else has defined or thinks is best. Once you've defined your 'all', as with your purpose, you have to think about choices and prices!

My 'all' is big. So I know I have to rise to the occasion. For example, I need to be in peak physical condition to have the energy for my children and husband, and I need to be healthy to actually be there for them – so this means I choose exercise and I have to keep trying to eat well. I want us all to be close, so I have to choose to spend time with them and prioritize them (e.g. bedtime routine, set up like appt, saying YES to my husband or to any opportunity to spend time with him).

What do you need to choose to have your 'all'?

_____

_____

_____

_____

What do you need to choose more of to have your 'all'? (I need to have more PATIENCE, and stop bringing my tired self to storytime – I am now falling asleep as soon as they start to read, so I need to start that earlier)

_____

_____

_____

_____

What do you need to SWERVE entirely to have your 'all'? (I have to say more NO's to requests on my time, so I have more time and energy for my 'all')

_____

_____

_____

_____

What is the price you have to pay to have your 'all'? (I can't be the best at everything at the same time, so I give up that need, I make trade-offs repeatedly, I give up my need to control because for relationships to thrive they require compromise)

_____

_____

_____

_____

'BALANCE'

I don't know what 'balance' really means – instead of worrying about what it means and whether I am doing it, I define my all, decide on my priorities, decide HOW I want to show up in my relationships and then do the BEST that I can. I know for sure that life occurs in seasons – when I had no children, I was in a particular season (and I worked like a FIEND), when I had a newborn I worked and slept less, when its college admission deadline time I work longer hours, but no matter what I always try to keep the priorities (kids/husband) the priorities – and I rebalance when I fall short. I don't want them to be the balls that drop (well I don't want any balls to drop, but those CANNOT drop!). The consequences of not being there for and with my family, not building close relationships with them and spending the time required to do that, well those are consequences I am not prepared to face. I don't want to be winning in my career and crushing my goals … alone. In setting up my schedule and life I am building that time in. When it's decision time, I remember what the priority is. What truly fills me up and brings me joy and makes me so, so happy - my family. My mentor, CEO of a large, global power company, Kelly Tomblin-Morgan told me once that when you're being the best mom you may not be the best boss at that time - and any of the other combinations or iterations of your many roles. I police / observe myself and when I am working too much and not spending enough time with family I rebalance. \

My friend Nicola Melhado gave me the great advice to plan family vacations or activities whenever the children have time off from school. I made that my 2018 resolution and I've kept it. We have had great adventures together! We have decided to spend more time together discovering Jamaica, going for drives together. We've bought board games and play them together as a family – and I think we have been able to both have fun and teach valuable lessons to our kids over Monopoly! We eat together on Sundays, but need to work on eating together more often because the BEST conversations happen around the table. Our schedules are all so different, but, no excuses I am working on that as a top priority. How can you build your family time into your schedule? In the Chapter on Choosing Support I will talk more about how habits, automation and routine save me! If it's scheduled, becomes habit and is part of your routine then it flows and you don't have to feel like you are always exerting effort, it just happens!

What are some rituals / routine activities you can build in with your family?

_____

_____

_____

_____

Doing the best I can, keeping my priorities my priorities and accepting that I can't be everything at the same time is my 'balance'. In doing the best that I can I tell myself that it is ALL possible, and I need to do everything that I can to rise to the occasion of my 'all'. I have to expand my personal capacity. It means I am constantly conscious AND aggressive about my time – I understand the value of it for myself and others, I am always seeking to learn how to **uplevel my clarity, organization, productivity (cut procrastination), efficiency, focus, return on investment, it means choosing my activities and projects carefully, it means choosing automation and systemization and it means choosing and investing in support (aggressively**). I invest in books, courses, conferences, mentors, google to learn how to do all those things better. I recognize that I have to get more done on truly meaningful and specific goals in less time. It means choosing ME with constant prayer, energy-generating activities like exercise and work I am passionate about, and choosing rest.

What are some of the things / areas you need to uplevel to expand your capacity?

_____

_____

_____

_____

Choosing Support – Systems & People

Choosing support and creating systems and routine allow me to 'balance', that is, do the best I can with everything in front of me. Choosing routine means my life flows easier and I can save my energy for high value tasks. Choosing systems means that a million things can be happening and no balls (or less balls) are dropping. I've been guided in this area a lot, again by my most 'UNreasonable' friend Nicola whom when I told that we could not afford to hire she responded by letting me know I couldn't afford NOT to! And boy was she right. She does not do reasons, she does action – that is why I call her UNreasonable. I live in Jamaica of course where the cost of labor compared to many other countries is much lower. So, we are blessed to be able to afford help in our home. My sister Anya lives in Canada, and pays a HUGE price and she makes the sacrifice as much as she is able to. It is not so much a sacrifice as it is an investment in expanding capacity to earn. At that point it becomes about doing the math - and the math may turn out differently than what we think once we actually do it. I have been surprised to realize what I can make work when I actually do the math and tighten my belt in terms of spending in another area and using the time I get back to earn. But help in the home doesn't have to be hired. Where would I be without the help and support of my sister and mom who live close by?

Although they both work full time and have busy lives, I have moved my kids into their homes for a few days when I needed to - and she does the same!

Although women typically bear the burden of child-care as my children get older, I find that Jeffrey is incredibly hands on and although the concept of asking your own husband for help seems strange … I know that if I don't tell him what I need him to do he will assume that superwoman Nicole has it all under control. Then I will resent that he isn't doing something. It goes back to clear communication we discussed earlier. When I read a Michelle Obama interview where she articulated that her marriage and life improved when she realized that all her help did not need to come from Barack … I embraced this FULLY, but when I need him to do things, I tell (I may make it sound like an ask, depending) him, very clearly.

Generally, I find that the more organized and systemized I am, the easier it is to run the house well, create more time and lessen stress. Everything is documented and easy to find from recipes to the kids' schedules. My monthly pharmacy list is set and only minor additions and subtractions need to be made – we know what we need every month why do we need to keep remembering and running out and forgetting and trying to remember? I send in my order and all the items are delivered by Fontana (Jamaica). I have things on Amazon – in Prime Pantry – that recur every 30 or 60 days depending. I constantly hunt for ways to automate so that I can spend my time on higher value tasks and activities like hanging out with my family, doing my nails, in my business, with my client etc. I choose my gym clothes the night before. I have set 'uniforms' for work that I created, and I just wear them over and over. The 3 or 4 shoes I always wear to work are lined up beside each other. I keep a kit in my car with makeup, a brush, hair gel, perfume – all I need to fix up before work (I need to leave early to beat the traffic and I don't usually have time to get cute, and I love cute!) and this kit comes in handy when I need to go to a function after work (who has the time to go home to change?). Small changes like this not only give you back your time, but they make life flow so that you can manage more without being harassed and running around! This is priceless for me!

What can you systemize, automate and / or document in your house or life to help things flow automatically?

_____

_____

_____

_____

_____

_____

I still have a FAR way to go and I am working on it. Other simple things for me have gone a long way, for example deciding what we will eat one week in advance and shopping accordingly. Meal prep, stick it in the fridge or freezer then toss it in the microwave. I ask for my assistant at work to be included in emails from my kids' teachers so I don't miss key things. At first, I felt a little ridiculous, but, I feel worse when I show up with my kids to school and they are wearing regular uniforms and everyone else is in PE clothes. There is no shame in asking for and accepting help (for me). You have to embrace what works FOR you. Still, at our last parent teacher conference our son's teacher pointed out that we needed to do better with tracking his assignments and school requirements. I agreed wholeheartedly and pledged to do better. I share this to say sometimes you are more on top of it than other times and you have to pull back or dig in accordingly. SO, I have added checking their bags and folders to our nightly bedtime routine. Problem solved by creating a routine.

What are the small things you're not on top of RIGHT NOW that you can build a routine around?

_____

_____

_____

_____

_____

_____

One of my mentors told me that you have to invest in additional employees before your business can actually afford it, in order to grow. I apply this principle aggressively in all areas of my life!

If you were to invest in help in your home or business, what would it free you up to achieve and earn?

_____

_____

_____

Some of you have no children or husband/wife yet – but these systems, adopted and implemented now will uplevel your self-management now which is a serious asset and skill no matter what your 'ALL' is, or what your future holds. Some of you are single parents who can't afford help and don't live near family. I can't pretend to walk in those shoes. It is tough. The truth is we each have our own unique circumstances and moments when meeting our goals in the midst of our current reality feels IMPOSSIBLE. Choosing though is about facing **the fact** that somewhere in the world, someone with less resources and more obstacles has found a way to achieve the seemingly impossible. And so must we. Our reality is our reality and we must challenge ourselves to maximize our potential no matter what. This is why I love to read stories of epic people and entrepreneurs who have built businesses and changed the world in the midst of terrible economies and personal circumstances.

I say, you can have your excuses and reasons (as legitimate as they are) or your results, but not both.

I choose results.

.

It isn't one thing all the time

Some days I feel like an entire failure. I wonder if I am doing it right. I wonder what I could be doing better. I feel like everyone else is further ahead or doing it better. I worry that I am not enough. I feel the weight and futility of trying to be the best mom, wife, daughter, friend, teacher, boss and self - ALL at the same time. The major key is deciding what your priorities are, and what being excellent means in those areas. o that you can identify when your energy and time is I tell myself EVERYDAY that I CAN. Even when I feel like my head is barely above water I tell myself I can. I know that there are so many hours in the day, and that if I commit to it, and continue to commit to it, work on my procrastination, work on my will and discipline, make the right choices about the time I do have… I KNOW like I KNOW that I can indeed accomplish more than perhaps someone with more hours to devote.

I say I CAN! I choose to recognize my reality, and try to maximize what I do have – and wherever that leaves me is where God means me to be. Somehow, I think this is one of the major keys to life, the fundamental principle that so many quotes and memes come from- it's that you make the best of what you have in front of you, which is yes, less time than someone with a less full life. But the delight of the full-ness! I would NEVER trade it for ANYTHING. I choose it. My mentee Chelsea shared that one of her favorite things to say to herself is, "I am exactly where I need to be," – I am going to use this to lessen my anxiety in the moments where choices and trade-offs must be made. I choose my life and I am so grateful.

I choose the love and the joy. I choose the chaos. I choose the tears. I choose the overwhelm. I choose the fear. I choose the anxiety. I choose the feelings of impossibility. I choose the hope. I choose the support. I choose the security. I choose the comfort. I choose the love. I choose it ALL.

6
CHOOSING OPTIMISM

Optimism is my biggest superpower and I believe one of the most life-altering choices one can make. When I say life-altering I literally mean it - studies show that optimism, that is, the belief that good things will happen in the future, can extend one's life span by almost 8 years[1]! I use the word **choice** deliberately - we must make the decision to see the glass as half full, to intercept half-empty thoughts and actively replace them with affirming thoughts about our present and our future. Optimism has improved the quality of my life, and when I catch myself not being optimistic I shift on purpose and I feel much happier, more creative and open to possibility. And it's not just me - optimism actually promotes the production of dopamine, dubbed the "ignition system" in our bodies, responsible for making us happy and increasing our motivation and courage![2] Dopamine is absolutely essential for our wellbeing and success, and choosing optimism is a natural way to put ourselves in the driver's seat of our own lives and success.

How I Choose Optimism

I am a self-professed "inspirational quote junkie" and I am so proud of it! I keep my brain on positive by filling my mind with inspirational quotes everyday - quotes on winning, losing and bouncing back, on joy, on peace. I love quotes so much I even made my own inspirational quotes Instagram page

---

[1] Brain Rules for Aging Well by Dr. John Medina
[2] Brain Science Reveals the Striking Power of Optimism by Carmine Gallo, Forbes Magazine Online

- @nicspire. Quotes give me strength when I need it, encourage me when I don't and I find so many of them, so easily, on Instagram.

Speaking of social media, I am very deliberate in terms of who I follow and don't follow! I find that what we feed our brains affects our mood and energy, which in turn affects our ability to flex our optimism muscles! After viewing the feeds of the people you follow do you mostly feel empowered? Excited? Filled with possibility? Are you drained?

Another strategy I use is self-talk, often out loud! People might think I am crazy but you might hear me saying "Nicole, get your mind right", "Nicole, no weapon formed!!" Or "What's the opportunity here?". The conversations we have with ourselves are the most important conversations we will ever have! So, I proudly speak to myself daily! I also pray, I thank the Lord for things that have not even happened yet! I pray with a spirit of positive expectancy and focus on all the winning ahead, that I can't even see, because I know for sure that what you focus on does multiply.

I also use music to help me choose optimism. Music is one of the most powerful tools that exist and it is ABSOLUTELY essential in my optimism toolkit. 'Winning Right Now' by Agent Sasco is one of my favorite songs ever, and when I listen to it I feel super optimistic! I have a playlist which includes other songs that inspire the same feeling, and I play them both when I'm happy and optimistic and when I'm down and fearful or anxious about the future.

VISIONBOARDING: *The Ultimate Expression of Optimism*

I have been vision boarding for almost 10 years and I believe so much in its power that I now train companies and individuals on Visionboarding - in person and on-line! Thinking carefully about what we want for our lives and putting images to foam board takes tremendous optimism since the future is not guaranteed, but one must force oneself to "see" one's future, in all it's glory, as though it has already happened. As I look at my 2018 Visionboard in amazement at all the things that have actually happened, I am so happy that I choose optimism daily.

Choosing to be optimistic, is an expression of courage. To believe that great things will happen in our future is to expose ourselves to the possibility that maybe it won't happen, and to the inevitable disappointment that comes with that. But life is happening to everyone and disappointment will come whether we are optimistic or not. The cost of NOT being optimistic though - increased susceptibility to depression which elevates the stress hormone cortisol in our bodies, compromising our immune systems and leaving us more susceptible to infectious diseases - is simply too high a price to pay for me. So I choose optimism instead. What you choose becomes your reality.

Choose powerfully.

CONCLUSION

I hope by now you are in the driver's seat, and if you were already in the driver's seat, I hope that you are even MORE in the driver's seat.

What an incredible delicious freedom I experienced when I stopped fearing that I wouldn't be "lucky" and set about designing and determining my life one choice at a time.

I wish I could jump on a mega phone and share it with the world. I wish that more than sharing it, I could make everyone in the world believe AND internalize AND live the MAJOR key truth:

Your life is up to you. And this is your one precious life, it is not a dress rehearsal for some other life. No one is coming to save you. You have to save yourself, and you have to do it now.

INSTA FRIENDS Q&A

How do I balance and mother wife and exercise? One or more has to give and its exercise right now.

First of all, please know that none have to give. If other women do it (like me and countless other women), you can do it, and do it WELL. So, put it in your mind that NOTHING has to give, and to be successful at anything you need to learn how other people successfully do the thing you seek to do. You can learn anything. You can build any skill. It is a matter of learning how they do it and then CHOOSING to do it. Are you willing to pay the price? It might mean getting up that much earlier. I recommend that you choose a time daily, where you do not have to actively, physically fulfill those roles of mom and wife - I exercise really early in the morning when I am sure that no one will need me at home or work because exercise is central to my wellbeing and productivity, it is not an option for me it is a must. When you put in your mind that something is not an option you find a way to do it. For me, the cost of NOT exercising is not a price that I am willing to pay (decreased energy and drive, less confidence etc).

How do you get folks to take you seriously about choosing the life you want

I don't worry about whether they will or not, I decide to be EXCELLENT at what I do, and then they have no choice but to take me seriously. I am not waiting on permission or approval. I take action and those speak for themselves.

On days when you get tired and frustrated what gives you that extra push to move forward

Well, sometimes, as I described earlier, I may not move forward, I may actually stop and rest. I am really learning to listen to my body in that way. If the fatigue and frustration are not signals of the need for rest, if they are actually situationally based then I share with a trusted confidante or person who can help (usually mom, sister, husband, colleague), vent a bit depending on who it is. and then brainstorm solutions / actions in order to solve the problem or improve the situation.

In the regular course of life when I am not tired and there is no particular situation but I just feel pop down and unmotivated I do NOT stop executing. I don't allow this feeling to take hold and plunge me into inaction and reduced productivity or overeating because I know that all of those things will only make me feel worse, so I flex my discipline muscle, I pray and exercise, I listen to my motivation music list and sing out loud, I keep my appointments and execute my tasks according to my lists, I tell myself "it is well" and this too shall pass, I am learning now to practice that self-compassion I talk about by telling myself to take it easy and reassuring myself that "this too shall pass".

What do you do when the resources are low to keep going?

I curb my spending and pray super super hard, breathe deeply and repeat, it is well. Also, I try to learn the lesson - why are resources so low? Is there something I can do avoid being in this position again? Do I need to cut my expenses or increase my income, or both? How can I do those things? This too shall pass I tell myself and remind myself that all the people who have found GREAT success have struggled in different ways, so, again, this too shall pass.

Is it normal for a 23-year-old to not know which career path to choose?

I don't know if it is normal and I don't think it matters. What matters is that you're committed to finding out - this means doing those exercises in the chapters above to get clarity on what excites you, searching for volunteer opportunities, interviewing people who are doing what you may be interested in doing, creating a vision board, figuring out how, even with your current job or responsibilities, you can do more of the thing or things that set you on fire, taking the first step without being able to see the staircase and of course, always, always acknowledging the price and deciding to pay it -whatever it may be.

ACKNOWLEDGEMENTS

Thank You God for placing dreams on my heart, for endless mercy when I fall short, for direction, wisdom and guidance. Thank You for helping me to hear Your voice.

My heart is so full – thank you to my social media community – you have driven me in so many ways and given me the vision for this book. Thank you to Chelsea Taylor for your perspective and feedback as I finalized the book. To my team at work and at home - your support is EVERYTHING!

Thank you of course to my friends and family who are a constant source of support and love and encouragement. Thank you to my bonus daughter Ally who inspires me with the quality choices she makes, and to my husband Jeffrey for choosing me.

To Joshua and Lauren - I keep trying to make the best choices because you exist, so thank you for simply being!

ABOUT THE AUTHOR

Nicole McLaren Campbell boasts a fiercely flourishing career as an entrepreneur, educator, and professional speaker and author. She is a graduate of the St Andrew High School for Girls, Phillips Academy 'Andover', Princeton University and the University of London's Schools of Advanced Study and African and Oriental Studies.

In 2010, she founded AIM Educational Services, which revolutionized the preparation of students for college - starting from just two students to guiding scores of students to the most prestigious universities in the world, including Oxford and Cambridge Universities in the United Kingdom and all 8 Ivy League institutions in the United States. AIM offers parents a return on investment of over 5000% when the cost of the program versus the average size scholarship AIM students receive. In 2018, Nicole founded Nicspire, an empowerment and success coaching business through which she trains individuals and businesses in improving personal productivity, creating vision boards and achieving their goals. She is also the founder of the AIM Higher Foundation with a mandate to identify, develop and empower promising low-income students so that they too can access unlock their potential through access to tertiary education. To that end, she serves on the Boards of the Early Childhood Commission, the HEART Trust/NTA, the Jamaica Tertiary Education Committee and the CHASE Fund in Jamaica.

In 2017 Nicole published her first book Make It Count: Tips on Unlocking Your Vision in 2017 and Beyond, which has now been revised to Make It Count: Tips on Unlocking Your Vision. Nicole's inspirational 'empowerment manual,' which aims to motivate readers to unlock their potential is driven by her unwavering belief that "Successful people aren't born that way, and with the right toolkit we can all do what successful people do."

Regarded as one of the most influential voices on empowerment, education, parenting and entrepreneurship, McLaren Campbell was selected to speak at the Paris Headquarters of UNESCO as part of the Give1 Foundation Emerging Global Leaders Conference and presented with their Women In Leadership Award in 2017 and this year recognized by the highest office in Jamaica, that of the Governor General, when she was named a 2018 recipient of the Governor General's Award for Excellence in Achievement and Leadership.

She is wife to Jeffrey, mom to 7-year old LC, 5-year-old Joshua and 'bonus-mom' to 12-year-old Ally. A self-professed inspirational quote junkie, her personal motto is "AIM High and Be Bold" and her mission is to squeeze every ounce of life, from life.

Follow her @nicolemclarencampbell on Instagram to see her life in action! For speaking engagements and workshops email bookings@nicolemclarencampbell.com.

Made in the USA
Lexington, KY
06 November 2019